Grace Lin  Ranida T. McKneally

Our Food

A Healthy Serving of Science and Poems

Peachtree

Illustrated by Grace Zong

i📖i Charlesbridge

Breakfast, lunch, dinner—
Every day, we eat and eat.
But I'm still hungry!

Why do we eat?

Your body is always using energy. Everything you do takes energy, even things you barely think about, like breathing and blinking. To run, bike, or swim, you definitely need lots of energy. Where does all this energy come from? Our food!

You can think of food as fuel for your body. The energy from this fuel is measured in calories. Some foods have more calories than others. Food also gives your body nutrients, the building blocks it needs to work properly. Some foods have a lot of nutrients; others have almost none.

Which foods help you stay strong and healthy? Knowing about the five food groups—and eating well—will help keep you going all day long.

The Five Food Groups

Fruits

Grains

Protein foods

Dairy

Vegetables

Fruits

First a little seed,
Then a flower, and a fruit,
To plant in my mouth!

What is a fruit?

A fruit is like a seed packet—it's the part of a flowering plant that holds the seeds. Fruits come in all shapes, sizes, and textures. They can be big and tall (pineapples) or round and small (grapes). They can feel firm (apples) or soft (berries). Some fruits have skin that's fuzzy (kiwis), bumpy (lychees), or even hairy (rambutans). Others, which may not seem like fruit to you, are dry and have a hard shell (peanuts).

Whether huge like a watermelon or tiny like a blueberry, fruits taste great and are filled with vitamins, minerals, and other nutrients. Fruits make terrific snacks, especially when you need a quick, healthy burst of flavor and energy.

What makes fruit sweet?

When you bite into a ripe, juicy peach, the sweetness from sugars in the fruit fills your mouth. Where do these sugars come from? Plants use sunlight, water, and carbon dioxide gas from the air to make sugars. The sugars are a kind of nutrient called carbohydrates and are high in energy. Plants use this energy to make stems grow, flowers bloom, and fruits ripen. When you eat the fruit, you get some of that energy.

Why are some fruits sour? As a fruit ripens, its mix of sweet sugars and sour acids changes. Unripe fruits usually have more acids and taste tart and sour. Ripe fruits have more sugars and taste sweeter. Some fruits, like oranges, taste sweet and sour at the same time.

Sweet, delicious peach,
Always where I cannot reach.
The birds laugh at me.

Red plums high above.
Red strawberries down below.
Red stains on my mouth!

Why are fruits so colorful?

Fruits turn softer, sweeter, and brighter as they ripen. The bright colors and sweet taste attract fruit-eating animals such as birds and squirrels. This is important for plants because these animals spread seeds. The seeds that drop as the animal eats—or that come out in the animal's poop later—can grow into new plants.

The color of a fruit gives us a clue to the nutrition in it. For example, orange fruits like apricots and cantaloupes are rich in beta-carotene, an orange pigment made by plants. Your body changes beta-carotene to vitamin A. This vitamin keeps your skin, eyes, and other body parts working the way they should. So choosing and snacking on fruits in a rainbow of colors is a brilliant way to keep your body healthy.

Vegetables

It's hard to believe:

They say tomatoes are fruits.

Not for my dessert!

What's the difference between a fruit and a vegetable?

We eat many delicious plant parts: leaves (lettuce), stems (asparagus), leaf stalks (celery), roots (carrots), bulbs (onions), flower buds (broccoli), and seeds (peas). You probably know most of these plant parts as "vegetables."

People usually eat vegetables for the main part of a meal. Fruits are sweeter, so we often eat them as desserts or snacks. But to scientists, many foods that people call "vegetables" are actually fruits, because they develop from flowers and hold the plant's seeds. Believe it or not, tomatoes, squash, and beans are actually fruits. Whether fruits or vegetables, foods from plants make your meals colorful. And the more kinds you eat, the better!

Why are so many vegetables green?

Many vegetables, like lettuce, brussels sprouts, and bok choy, are very green. The green color comes from a pigment called chlorophyll. Chlorophyll absorbs the sun's energy and uses it to make sugars. The plant then uses the sugars for energy. Green leaves packed with chlorophyll are like a plant's power stations. So when you eat leafy greens, just think of all that power you're getting.

Vegetables can be other colors, too. Farmers' markets are filled with reds and oranges (beets, yams), yellows and golds (summer squash, sweet corn), and blues and purples (blue corn, eggplants). Each color means a particular set of healthy nutrients. What vegetables come in your favorite color?

I wish I could grow
Beans that were not only green.
Dreams of jelly beans.

Rabbits are welcome
In the vegetable garden.
There's lettuce for all!

Why do I have to eat my vegetables?

Vegetables are full of vitamins and minerals. For example, leafy, dark-green "super vegetables" like kale and spinach are packed with vitamins A and C, and calcium. These nutrients help your eyes see well, your bones stay strong, and your cuts heal. Vegetables also provide carbohydrates for energy—without a lot of extra calories.

Vegetables have fiber, too. Fiber is the part of the plant that your body can't easily break down, like the strings of celery. After food enters your mouth, it moves along your digestive system, where your body takes in all the nutrients it can. What's left over comes out at the other end as poop. Eating enough fiber helps you poop normally, so you can stay comfortable!

Grains

How tall the corn grows!
Reaching up toward the sun,
Talking to scarecrows.

What makes a grain a grain?

When you eat grain you're eating the small, hard, dry fruits of tall grasses. Corn, wheat, rice, millet, and barley are grains. A grain kernel is made up of three parts. The bran on the outside is full of fiber, vitamins, and minerals. The germ, the part that grows into a new plant, is also packed with nutrients. The endosperm, the largest part, gives the young plant its food and energy.

Flour is ground-up grain. With flour you can make dough. You can knead dough into soft loaves or thin flatbreads such as tortillas. You can stretch it into soba noodles, shape it into rotini, or fill it to make samosas. Or you can eat grains just as they are. What grains have you eaten today?

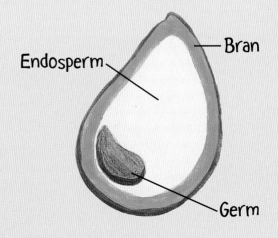

What's the difference between brown bread and white bread?

Some foods are made from whole grains, and others are made from not-so-whole grains. Whole grains are "whole" because they include all three parts of the grain: the bran, germ, and endosperm. Brown breads are usually made from whole grains. Their brown color and rough texture come from the outer layers of the grain. White breads are lighter in color and smoother. They are usually made from refined grains, or grains with the bran and germ removed.

All grains contain carbohydrates, which give you energy. But whole grains are the healthiest grains because they have more nutrients and fiber. So power up on whole grains! Your body will thank you for it.

Is there a difference
Between brown bread and white bread
Besides a toaster?

Those little kernels
Have big noises inside them.
Best cover your ears!

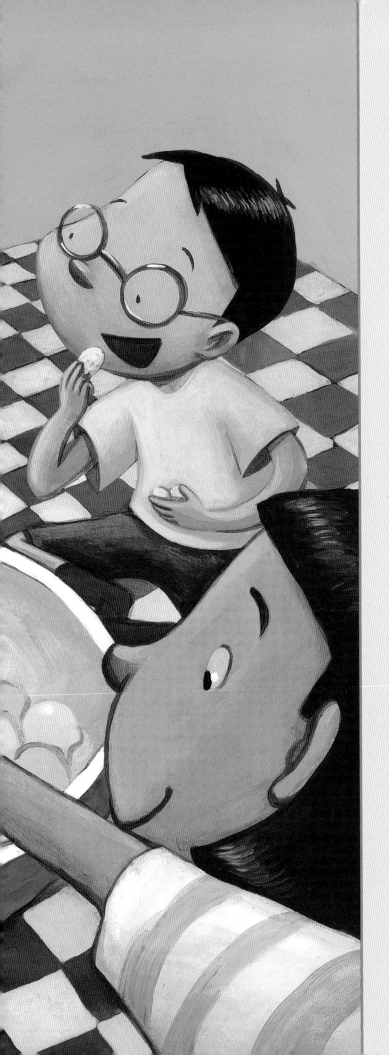

What makes popcorn pop?

Not just any kind of corn will pop. Popcorn is different from sweet corn on the cob. The bran around a popcorn kernel is very hard, and the endosperm inside is pretty hard, too. How does a small, hard kernel turn into a crispy fluff? The secret is water.

When you heat popcorn, the small amount of water inside the kernel turns to steam. The steam softens the endosperm and turns it into jelly. Trapped by the strong, hard shell, the steam can't escape, and pressure builds up inside. Eventually the pressure is so high that the shell cracks and—POP! The kernel bursts and the endosperm puffs out. So the next time you eat popcorn, just think: you're eating a kernel that has turned inside out!

Protein foods

I've always wondered:

Do brown chickens lay brown eggs?

My thoughts are scrambled.

What are protein foods?

Meat, poultry, seafood, eggs, beans, tofu, and nuts are all high in protein. Proteins are important building blocks for every part of your body. Your hair is mostly protein. Proteins in your muscles allow you to move. Proteins in your skin make it strong and waterproof. Your body also needs protein to repair itself.

Proteins are built from chemicals called amino acids. Your body can make about half of the amino acids it needs; the rest must come from food. Meat, fish, poultry, and eggs contain the full set of amino acids. You can also get the full set by eating a good mix of foods from plants. Just like you need all the letters of the alphabet to build words, your body needs all the amino acids to keep on building—you!

The color of an egg depends on the type of chicken, not on the color of the hen's feathers.

Almonds are "good fats"?
Do they fight crime in disguise?
Seems nutty to me.

Why are lean meats healthier than fatty meats?

Fat is a nutrient that your body needs for energy and for doing many important jobs, such as building your brain. Most foods have fats in them, but some fats are healthier than others. Eating too many "bad" fats may lead to some diseases when you grow older. Eating "good" fats may help protect against those diseases.

Protein foods from animals generally contain more bad fats than good fats. Chicken and turkey have fewer bad fats than red meats like beef and pork do, though. And fish has a lot of good fats. Other protein foods high in good fats include nuts, avocados, tofu, and beans. Choosing foods with good fats will help your body keep on going strong.

"Good" fats

"Bad" fats

That big bowl of beans
Is now completely empty.
Stay away from me!

Why do beans make you gassy?

Beans are a great source of protein. They tend to make you a little gassy, though. Passing gas is completely normal and happens for different reasons—but what is it about beans?

Beans are coated with a type of sugar that your body can't easily break down. Your body needs help from bacteria, living things so small you need a microscope to see them. Bacteria live everywhere—including in your large intestine, the last part of your digestive system. There the bacteria digest the beans' sugars and fiber—and give off lots of gas. Fortunately, the gas that comes from eating beans is not the really stinky kind!

Dairy

In the summertime
Don't forget to thank the cows
When you eat ice cream.

What is milk?

Many foods come from milk, including butter, cheese, yogurt, kefir, and ice cream. But where does milk come from? Like all mammals, dairy animals such as cows, goats, and sheep make milk to feed their babies. Milk contains nutrients that help the young animals grow up strong and healthy. The nutrients in milk can also help keep human bodies healthy.

Milk is made of proteins, sugars, fats, vitamins, minerals, and lots of water. One important mineral is calcium. Your body uses calcium to build strong bones and teeth, make your muscles move, and stop wounds from bleeding.

Most of the milk you see at the store is cow's milk. In other parts of the world, people also drink milk from yaks, camels, and even reindeer.

What's the difference between whole milk and skim milk?

Whether milk comes in a jug, carton, or bottle, it can be whole, reduced-fat, or skim. What does that mean? Before milk is ready for the store, it has to be prepared at a dairy plant. There the milk is cleaned and treated to destroy harmful bacteria. Its amount of natural fat, called butterfat, can also be changed.

Whole milk has all of the butterfat in it. Reduced-fat milk has some of the butterfat removed. Skim milk has almost no fat in it at all; it is also called fat-free milk. Cheese, yogurt, and other dairy products can be made with milk that is whole, skim, or somewhere in between.

We stir and we watch.

In the pot, milk swirls around.

When will this be cheese?

Smelling like old socks,
The cheese makes my nose wrinkle.
But I'm eating it!

Why are some cheeses so stinky?

Cheese can be soft, hard, lumpy, stringy, holey, white, yellow, or even blue. Some cheeses, like mozzarella and cheddar, smell just fine. Others, such as feta, smell a bit more. Then there are *really* stinky cheeses with fun names like Limburger, Roquefort, and Stinking Bishop.

Making cheese involves curdling milk—separating it into solids (curds) and liquid (whey). The curds can then be pressed and shaped into cheese. To help with the curdling, cheese makers usually add bacteria or molds to the milk. As the bacteria and molds break down the milk, they give off a stinky smell. So it's thanks to tiny invisible microbes that we have the big flavors—and smells—of cheese.

The "blue" in blue cheeses like Gorgonzola is actually mold!

My plate is magic.
Fill it with favorite foods,
And they disappear!

Let's eat!

Knowing about the different food groups helps you make good decisions about what to eat. You need enough calories to get you through the day, but not too many. Foods with the same amount of calories can be packed with nutrients (fruits and vegetables) or have few to no nutrients at all (junk food and sweets). What's better for your body? You can be sure that foods with more nutrients will help you keep going longer and stay in better shape.

In general, try to eat plenty of fruits and vegetables, the more kinds and colors the better. Choose whole grains like whole-wheat bread and brown rice. Eat healthy proteins like fish, poultry, and beans. Make sure you get enough calcium from milk or other sources like broccoli, tofu, and beans. Drinking lots of water and avoiding sugary drinks are good ideas, too. And it can be fun exploring new foods—just be sure to avoid foods made with ingredients that you are allergic to if you have food allergies.

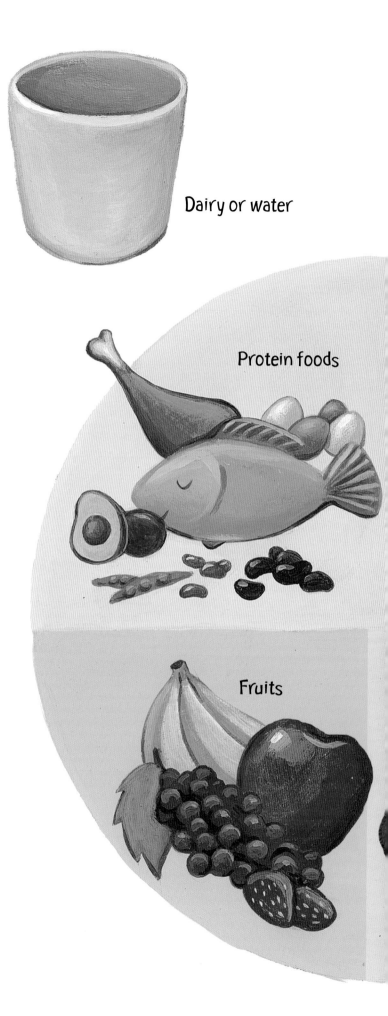

Dairy or water

Protein foods

Fruits

What does a healthy meal look like?

Different groups recommend different eating guidelines. For example, the United States Department of Agriculture recommends including skim or 1% milk with each meal, while the Harvard School of Public Health suggests drinking water instead.

In general, though, you can think of each meal as a divided plate: about a quarter vegetables, a quarter fruits, a quarter whole grains, and a quarter healthy protein.

So are beans fruits, vegetables, or proteins?

You've probably noticed that some foods belong to more than one food group. For example, beans are technically fruits, but they are usually grouped with vegetables or proteins. As vegetables, beans provide important vitamins, minerals, and fiber. As proteins, they contain the building blocks your body uses to build your hair, toenails, and everything in between.

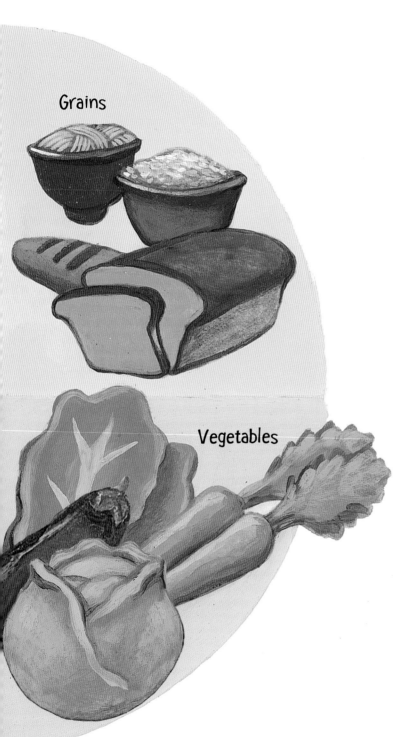

Grains

Vegetables

How will you power your body?

Feeding your body nutritious foods helps you think and focus during activities like reading, drawing, and playing the piano. It also gives you the energy to play soccer, dance, and do other physical activities. Staying active goes hand in hand with eating well—healthy foods fuel your body for physical activity, and physical activity helps your body work better. What power foods are you going to eat next?

Glossary

amino acid: A building block of protein. Your body can make some amino acids, but others have to come from food.

bacteria: Tiny organisms (living things) too small to see but everywhere around us.

beta-carotene: A reddish-orange pigment made by plants that your body turns into vitamin A.

bran: The outer layer of a kernel of grain.

calcium: A mineral the body needs for muscle movement, blood flow, bone growth, and many other processes.

calorie: A measurement of the amount of energy in food.

carbohydrate: A major nutrient and your body's main source of energy. Carbohydrates include natural sugars and starches found in fruits, vegetables, and grains, as well as sugars added to foods.

chlorophyll: A green pigment that allows plants to make their own food using the sun's energy.

endosperm: The largest part of a grain kernel, and the food supply for the developing plant.

energy: The ability to do work, from moving your muscles (energy from food) to boiling a pot of water (heat energy).

fat: A major nutrient that is high in energy.

fiber: The parts of a plant that people cannot digest.

fruit: The part of a flowering plant that holds the seeds.

germ: The part inside a grain kernel that grows into a new plant.

grain: The small, dry, hard fruits of tall, grassy plants such as corn, wheat, and rice.

microbe: A tiny organism (living thing) not visible to the eye.

mineral: A nutrient that your body needs in small amounts. Minerals come from the earth and are absorbed through food.

mold: A type of organism (living thing) that often grows as fuzzy strands.

nutrient: A substance in food that the body needs to grow, develop, and work normally. Vitamins, minerals, proteins, and carbohydrates are all nutrients.

pigment: A chemical that gives plant and animal cells (such as those in leaves and skin) color.

protein: A major nutrient important for building and repairing the body. Proteins are made up of amino acids.

vegetable: A plant or plant part that people eat as food.

vitamin: A nutrient that the body needs in only tiny amounts but is necessary for the body to work normally. Vitamins are made by plants and animals.

whole grain: A grain or food that includes all three parts of the grain kernel (bran, germ, and endosperm).

whole milk: Milk with all its natural butterfat.

To my friend Libby Koponen and the delicious (and mostly healthy) lunches we have eaten together.

—G. L.

To Amah and Nonna, for all the yummy, healthy meals you feed us!

—R. T. M.

To my sister, Jessica, who feeds me all the time!

—G. Z.

Special thanks to Dr. Esther Hee Jin Kim, ScD, RD, LDN, for her invaluable expertise and advice. Dr. Kim received her doctorate from the Harvard School of Public Health and has been a practicing dietitian for more than fifteen years.

Published by Charlesbridge
85 Main Street
Watertown, MA 02472
(617) 926-0329
www.charlesbridge.com

Library of Congress Cataloging-in-Publication Data
Lin, Grace, author.
   Our food / Grace Lin and Ranida T. McKneally; illustrated by Grace Zong.
      pages cm
   Includes bibliographical references and index.
   ISBN 978-1-58089-590-3 (reinforced for library use)
   ISBN 978-1-60734-844-3 (ebook)
   ISBN 978-1-60734-845-0 (ebook pdf)
1. Food—Juvenile literature. 2. Nutrition—Juvenile literature.
3. Diet—Juvenile literature. I. McKneally, Ranida, author.
II. Zong, Grace, illustrator. III. Title.

TX355.L47 2016
613.2—dc23   2015020212

Printed in China
(hc) 10 9 8 7 6 5 4 3 2 1

Illustrations done in acrylic on paper
Display type set in Ogre by Adobe Systems Incorporated
Text type set in Caslon by Adobe Systems Incorporated
Color separations by Colourscan Print Co Pte Ltd, Singapore
Printed by 1010 Printing International Limited in Huizhou,
   Guangdong, China
Production supervision by Brian G. Walker
Designed by Susan Mallory Sherman and Diane M. Earley